At Home Away

....

At Home Away

....

Devotions for Students

....

Carl W. Berner

....

CPH
SAINT LOUIS

CONTENTS

III. Prayers

Introduction

The next time you drive through a residential area, notice the colorful wind socks and decorative flags that many families hang outside their homes. Then imagine that four large banners fly over your house, apartment, or dorm:

Here God's Word Is Honored

Here Love Prevails

Here Truth Triumphs

Here Faith Abounds

This idea of banners may seem a bit strange, but it comes from the Bible: "You have raised a banner to be unfurled against the bow" (Psalm 60:4); "His banner over me is love (Song of Songs 2:4); "You are ... majestic as troops with banners" (Song of Songs 6:4); "We will shout for joy when You are victorious and will lift up our banners in the name of our God" (Psalm 20:5).

As we explore these four banner themes, you will find much that will lead to a fuller life for you. This is an exciting time! Wherever your studies and career and family life take you, may you always be able to say proudly about your home, "God's banner flies here!"

PART I

A Primer in the Christian Life

Show me Your ways, O LORD,
teach me Your paths.
Psalm 25:4

The Banner of God's Word

By announcing that "here God's Word is honored," you are taking an important step toward a fuller life. Our heavenly Father says this about His Word: "All Scripture is God-breathed and is useful for teaching, rebuking, correcting and training in righteousness, so that the man [and woman] of God may be thoroughly equipped for every good work" (2 Timothy 3:16–17).

Psalm 119:9 asks this question: How can young people keep their way pure? It then offers this answer: "By living according to Your [God's] Word." In response to the redeeming work of Jesus, we look to God's Word for guidance of how to live a pure life. If one's life is Word-centered, it will be rich, abundant, and true. No force in this world has done as much good, given as much light, brought so much happiness, dried as many tears, spread so much righteousness, gladdened as many hearts, as has the Holy Spirit, working through the precious Word of God.

The Bible, the inspired Word of God, can be a constant source of inspiration, guidance, and reproach. Here is a quick sampling of the breadth of wisdom found in the Scriptures.

An Alphabet of the Word

All have sinned and fall short of the glory of God. (Romans 3:23)

By grace you have been saved, through faith—and this not from yourselves, it is the gift of God. (Ephesians 2:8)

Come to Me, all you who are weary and burdened, and I will give you rest. (Matthew 11:28)

Delight yourself in the LORD, and He will give you the desires of your heart. (Psalm 37:4)

Enter through the narrow gate. For wide is the gate and broad is the road that leads to destruction, and many enter through it. (Matthew 7:13)

Faith is being sure of what we hope for and certain of what we do not see. (Hebrews 11:1)

God so loved the world that He gave His one and only Son, that whoever believes in Him shall not perish but have eternal life. (John 3:16)

Honor the LORD with your wealth, with the firstfruits of all your crops. (Proverbs 3:9)

I [Jesus] am the way and the truth and the life. No one comes to the Father except through Me. (John 14:6)

Jesus Christ is the same yesterday and today and forever. (Hebrews 13:8)

Keep me as the apple of Your eye; hide me in the shadow of Your wings. (Psalm 17:8)

Love each other as I have loved you. (John 15:12)

My son, if sinners entice you, do not give in to them. (Proverbs 1:10)

Not everyone who says to Me, "Lord, Lord," will enter the kingdom of heaven, but only he who does the will of My Father who is in heaven. (Matthew 7:21)

O LORD my God, I will give You thanks forever. (Psalm 30:12)

Pray continually. (1 Thessalonians 5:17)

Quiet words of the wise are more to be heeded than the shouts of a ruler of fools. (Ecclesiastes 9:17)

Repent and be baptized, every one of you, in the name of Jesus Christ for the forgiveness of your sins. And you will receive the gift of the Holy Spirit. (Acts 2:38)

Scripture says, "Anyone who trusts in Him will never be put to shame." (Romans 10:11)

Turn my eyes away from worthless things; preserve my life according to Your word. (Psalm 119:37)

Understand that no prophecy of Scripture came about by the prophet's own interpretation. For prophecy never had its origin in the will of man, but men spoke from God as they were carried along by the Holy Spirit. (2 Peter 1:20–21)

Vindicate me by Your might. Hear my prayer, O God; listen to the words of my mouth. (Psalm 54:1–2)

We know that in all things God works for the good of those who love Him, who have been called according to His purpose. (Romans 8:28)

EXalt the LORD our God and worship at His footstool; He is holy. (Psalm 99:5)

You are my hiding place; You will protect me from trouble and surround me with songs of deliverance. (Psalm 32:7)

Zeal for Your house will consume me. (John 2:17)

....

There's a lot to discover in the Bible! Billy Sunday, an evangelist in the early part of this century, put it this way:

> The Word takes you into the Old Testament art galleries there to examine portraits of Noah, Abraham, Isaac, Jacob, Moses, Daniel, and other great friends of God. It leads you into the music room of the Psalms, where the

Holy Spirit sweeps the keyboard of divine truth until every reed and pipe in God's great organ vibrates with heavenly song. It takes you into the gardens of Ecclesiastes and the Song of Solomon to enjoy the fragrance of the Rose of Sharon and the scented spices of the Lily of the Valley. In the observatory room of the prophets you will gaze through the telescopes of prophecy pointing to far off events, all centering in the bright Morning Star. In the audience room of the King of Kings you will catch the vision of the glory of the Lord through the pen of Matthew, Mark, Luke, John. Then you will be taken into the correspondence room where Paul and Peter and James and John penned their immortal epistles. Lastly, you will enter the throne room of Revelation to get a glimpse of the fierce and final conflict between Christ and Satan, a preview of the bejeweled city, and a vision of the coronation of the King of kings and the Lord of lords. Then you will fall down in adoration before Him whose is the kingdom, the power, and the glory forever.

The president of Harvard University, Joseph Willard, said in his 1799 commencement address,

I hope and trust that you will all be believers in that sacred code called the Bible ... May your minds be strongly impressed with gratitude to God and His Son, the blessed

Redeemer, for the display of love, goodness, mercy and grace exhibited in this gospel.

And finally, these words of Dwight Moody come to mind:

> This book [the Bible] contains the mind of God, the state of man, the way of salvation, the doom of sinners, and the happiness of believers. Its doctrines are holy, its precepts are binding, its histories are true, and its decisions are immutable.

Read the Bible in order to be wise, believe it in order to be safe, and practice it in order to be holy. It contains light to direct you, food to support you, and comfort to cheer you. It is the traveler's map, the pilgrim's staff, the pilot's compass, the soldier's sword, and the Christian's charter. Here the gates of hell are revealed, paradise is restored, and heaven is opened.

The Banner of Love

"This is how God showed His love among us: He sent His one and only Son into the world that we might live through Him. ... If we love one another, God lives in us and His love is made complete in us" (1 John 4:9, 12).

Nothing makes Christianity so attractive as love in action. A good way to do this is to make every contact with every person a love contact.

The early believers knew the love it took for God to send His only Son to die for their—for *our*—sins. Their response was loving service to mankind. They knew that only through love could they share the Good News of God in Christ so that more people might be added to the rolls of eternal glory.

Believers today respond in much the same was by weaving into the fabric of their time worthwhile activities in the service of God and humanity so those they serve might be open to receive the Gospel. God is delighted when His children fill every page of their life with singing faith, joyful praise, radiant hope, loving service. Consider every day as an opportunity to practice love.

1 Corinthians 13 (the love chapter) explains it

best: "Love is patient, love is kind. It does not envy, it does not boast, it is not proud. It is not rude, it is not self-seeking, it is not easily angered, it keeps no record of wrongs. Love does not delight in evil but rejoices with the truth. ... Now these three remain: faith, hope and love. But the greatest of these is love" (verses 4–6, 13).

"Whoever does not love does not know God, because God is love" (1 John 4:8). This really tells the truth about us. "By this all men will know that you are My disciples, if you love one another" (John 13:35).

Take a good long look at Romans 13:8: "Let no debt remain outstanding, except the continuing debt to love one another, for he who loves his fellowman has fulfilled the law."

The Banner of Truth

Jesus once said, "I am the way and the truth and the life" (John 14:6). He also said, "For this reason I was born, and for this I came into the world, to testify to the truth" (John 18:37). "Then you will know the truth, and the truth will set you free" (John 8:32).

Knowing this truth brings triumph and victory over sin, death, and the devil. God's Word offers us the guarantee that what we believe is 100 percent absolutely true.

The truth that Christians believe is summarized in the great declaration called the Apostles' Creed. Here is that creed, or belief, with a commentary from the great reformer Martin Luther.

The Apostles' Creed

The First Article

I believe in God, the Father Almighty, Maker of heaven and earth.

What does this mean? I believe that God has made me and all creatures; that He has given me my body and soul, eyes, ears, and all my members, my reason and all my senses, and still takes care of them.

He also gives me clothing and shoes, food and drink, house and home, wife and children, land, animals, and all I have. He richly and daily provides me with all that I need to support this body and life.

He defends me against all danger and guards and protects me from all evil.

All this He does only out of fatherly, divine goodness and mercy, without any merit or worthiness in me. For all this it is my duty to thank and praise, serve and obey Him.

This is most certainly true.

The Second Article

And in Jesus Christ, His only Son, our Lord, who was conceived by the Holy Spirit, born of the Virgin Mary, suffered under Pontius Pilate, was crucified, died and was buried. He descended into hell. The third day He rose again from the dead. He ascended into heaven and sits at the right hand of God, the Father Almighty. From thence He will come to judge the living and the dead.

What does this mean? I believe that Jesus Christ, true God, begotten of the Father from eternity, and also true man, born of the Virgin Mary, is my Lord,

who has redeemed me, a lost and condemned person, purchased and won me from all sins, from death, and from the power of the devil; not with gold or silver, but with His holy, precious blood and with His innocent suffering and death,

that I may be His own and live under Him in His kingdom and serve Him in everlasting righteousness, innocence, and blessedness,

just as He is risen from the dead, lives and reigns to all eternity.

This is most certainly true.

The Third Article

I believe in the Holy Spirit, the holy Christian church, the communion of saints, the forgiveness of sins, the resurrection of the body, and the life everlasting. Amen

What does this mean? I believe that I cannot by my own reason or strength believe in Jesus Christ, my Lord, or come to Him; but the Holy Spirit has called me by the Gospel, enlightened me with His gifts, sanctified and kept me in the true faith.

In the same way He calls, gathers, enlightens, and sanctifies the whole Christian church on earth, and keeps it with Jesus Christ in the one true faith.

In this Christian Church He daily and richly forgives all my sins and the sins of all believers.

On the Last Day He will raise me and all the dead, and give eternal life to me and all believers in Christ.

This is most certainly true.

The creed is a wonderful, concise statement of faith that we may memorize and use in our Christian witness.

Another source of truth for the Christian is God's Law as given to us in the Ten Commandments. Here's a new paraphrase along with Martin Luther's comments on them.

The Ten Commandments (for Today)

I. **Never worship any other god.**

What does this mean? We should fear, love, and trust in God above all things.

II. **Never use the name of the Lord your God carelessly.**

What does this mean? We should fear and love God so that we do not curse, swear, use satanic arts, lie, or deceive by His name, but call upon it in every trouble, pray, praise, and give thanks.

III. **Remember the day of worship by observing it as a holy day.**

What does this mean? We should fear and love God so that we do not despise preaching and His Word, but hold it sacred and gladly hear and learn it.

IV. **Honor your father and your mother.**

What does this mean? We should fear and love God so that we do not despise or anger our parents and other authorities, but honor them, serve and obey them, love and cherish them.

V. **Never murder.**

What does this mean? We should fear and love God so that we do not hurt or harm our neighbor in his body, but help and support him in every physical need.

VI. **Never commit adultery.**

What does this mean? We should fear and love God so that we lead a sexually pure and decent life in what we say and do, and husband and wife love and honor each other.

VII. **Never steal.**

What does this mean? We should fear and love God so that we do not take our neighbor's money or possessions, or get them in any dishonest way, but help him to improve and protect his possessions and income.

VIII. **Never lie.**

What does this mean? We should fear and love God so that we do not tell lies about our neighbor, betray him, slander him, or hurt his reputation, but defend him, speak well of him, and explain everything in the kindest way.

IX. **Never desire to take someone else's household.**

What does this mean? We should fear and love God so that we do not scheme to get our neighbor's inheritance or house, or get it in a way which only appears right, but help and be of service to him in keeping it.

X. **Never desire to take another person's spouse—or anything else.**

What does this mean? We should fear and love God so that we do not entice or force away our neighbor's wife, workers, or animals, or turn them against him, but urge them to stay and do their duty.

In these Ten Commandments we have God's holy Law. The Law has this verdict: "You are a sinner!" The Gospel shouts, "You have a Savior!"

In the Law we see our total loss due to sin. But there is good news! In the Gospel we see our complete redemption through Christ Jesus. One way He gives this to us is in our Baptism.

Holy Baptism

Before Jesus ascended into heaven, He spoke these words to His disciples: "Go and make disciples of all nations, baptizing them in the name of the Father and of the Son and of the Holy Spirit" (Matthew 28:19).

What joy it is to be able to confidently and thankfully say, "I am a redeemed, baptized, forgiven, loved, cherished, honored son or daughter of Christ; purified by faith; joined to Christ by Baptism. I am a new person, living a new life in Christ, on my way to a new life.

All this is mine through my faith in the Lord Jesus Christ, whom I resolve to love and serve.

Holy Communion

Greek Christians speak of Holy Communion as "The Mystery" —and a great mystery it is! Early Christians spoke of it as a love feast. We often call it Holy Communion, the holy union between bread and Christ's body, and wine and our Lord's blood. We also call it communion because in it we are united with each other: "Because there is one loaf, we, who are many, are one body, for we all partake of the one loaf" (1 Corinthians 10:17).

Why do we celebrate Communion?

1. To receive our Lord's body and blood for the forgiveness of our sins. "He Himself bore our sins in His body on the tree" (1 Peter 2:24).

2. To proclaim and confess our faith in Jesus' death as the source of our life. "For whenever you eat this bread and drink this cup, you proclaim the Lord's death until He comes" (1 Corinthians 11:26).

3. Here we have a living memorial of what Jesus did to redeem us. "Do this in remembrance of Me" (Luke 22:19).

4. When our Lord said "Do this," He encouraged us to receive the Sacrament of Holy Communion frequently.

5. Holy Communion offers us very rich blessings. If Jesus would offer us a gold nugget or a diamond at His Holy Supper, every communion rail would be crowded. What He offers is worth far more: forgiveness, life, and salvation.

God wants us to be aware not only of our total loss in sin, but also of our complete forgiveness. We approach the altar in prayer:

> O almighty God, merciful Father, I, a poor, miserable sinner, confess to You all my sins and iniquities with which I have ever offended You and justly deserved Your punishment now and forever. But I am heartily sorry for them and sincerely repent of them, and I pray You of Your boundless mercy and for the sake of the holy, innocent, bitter sufferings and death of Your beloved Son, Jesus Christ, to be gracious and merciful to me, a poor sinful being (*LW*, p. 136).

> Leaving the table, we say,

> Lord Jesus, now You are in me and I am in You. Glory, hallelujah!

We should develop the habit of mentally and spiritually preparing for Communion by examining our hearts, acknowledging that we are sinners, and by seeking forgiveness. Then we can go out with renewed strength for a holier life.

6. In Communion, we receive a foretaste of heaven. Our union with Jesus here is the beginning of our eternal union with Him in heaven.

The Lord's Prayer

Our Father who art in heaven, hallowed be Thy name, Thy kingdom come, Thy will be done on earth as it is in heaven. Give us this day our daily bread; and forgive us our trespasses as we forgive those who trespass against us; and lead us not into temptation, but deliver us from evil. For Thine is the kingdom and the power and the glory forever and ever. Amen.

Jesus gave us this prayer. We may regard it as the best of all prayers, for it encompasses our every need. (Be careful not to make the mistake of slipping into the habit of saying it mechanically, without thinking.)

Look first at the "Thy" phrases. "Hallowed be *Thy* name, *Thy* kingdom come, *Thy* will be done." We pray that the name of God Himself may be held in highest regard; that His kingdom may prosper everywhere; that His good and holy will may be honored and respected.

Now let us look at the "us" phrases. We pray that He will continue to give *us* our daily bread, that He will not allow *us* to be led into temptation, and that He will deliver *us* from all evil in our lives.

The prayer ends by reflecting on those things that are His: *Thine* is the kingdom, *Thine* is the power, and *Thine* is the glory—may God the supreme one be exalted. What a prayer this is!

In this prayer we are asking God to equip us with weapons equal to those of the enemy. This is God's world, but there is a lot of enemy territory in it. We're living in rattlesnake country, and we had better walk cautiously. The devil will lay snares, set traps, place delays. He is highly resourceful, desperately wicked, very deceitful. A furious argument, a temper tantrum, a clever lawsuit, may suddenly engulf us in confusion, darkness, bitterness. Many a person has left home whistling and returned to it weeping. Therefore, we beseech God, "Lead us not into temptation, but deliver us from evil." We ask Him to take us by the hand, to equip us with faith and wisdom, and to lead us into the paths of righteousness.

He will answer our prayer. Our enemies are His enemies. He knows how to lead us safely through fields that are mined. He offers us many prayer "shelters."

Never forget this: The Lord Jesus Christ has achieved victory over the enemy of the human race: Satan and his fury, sin and its curse, death and its darkness. These all lie at his feet. Evil has met its master in

Jesus Christ, the mighty conqueror, who is with us and for us.

In all the darkness that surrounds us, He who is light and in whom "there is no darkness at all" (1 John 1:5) has power to keep us on the path of light and life.

Prayer: My dear Lord, grant me grace to seek and do Your will. Sweep out of my heart all evil: selfishness, grudge bearing, vengeance, pride. Fill my heart with all that is holy and good: faith, love, joy, peace, trust, hope, righteousness—all to Your glory and my present and eternal benefit. Amen.

The Banner of Faith

What is your favorite passage from the Bible? Psalm 1? Psalm 23, the Good Shepherd psalm? 1 Corinthians 13, the love chapter? Hebrews 11, the faith chapter? Or are you still new to the Bible, still seeking a favorite?

My favorite passage is a magnificent one that describes faith and what it does:

> Praise be to the God and Father of our Lord Jesus Christ! In His great mercy He has given us **new birth** into a **living hope** through the resurrection of Jesus Christ from the dead, and into an **inheritance** that can never perish, spoil or fade—kept in heaven for you, who through faith are **shielded by God's power** until the coming of the salvation that is ready to be revealed in the last time.

> In this you greatly **rejoice**, though now for a little while you may have had to suffer grief in all kinds of trials. These have come so that your **faith**—of greater worth than gold, which perishes even though refined by fire—may be proved genuine and may result in praise, glory and honor when Jesus Christ is revealed.

Though you have not seen Him, **you love Him**; and even though you do not see Him now, **you believe in Him** and are filled with an inexpressible and glorious **joy**, for you are receiving the goal of your faith, the **salvation of your souls** (1 Peter 1:3–9).

What power Christ has! In Christ Jesus, through faith, we can break through the strongest barriers as though they were spider's webs. In Christ, through faith, we can stand victorious over every adversity.

Jesus conquered sin and its consequences. This victory is witnessed in the lives of those who have faith in Him. When Jesus gave sight to the blind beggar Bartimaeus, Jesus said to him, "Your faith has healed you" (Mark 10:52). When a leper who had been cured came back to Jesus to thank Him, Jesus said, "Your faith has made you well" (Luke 17:19). Spiritual winters are turned into spring when we take Christ at His word and look to Him for every need. "This is the victory that has overcome the world, even our faith" (1 John 5:4).

Consider also the lives of all those listed in the faith chapter, Hebrews 11. Note how the author starts talking about each hero:

By faith Abel … By faith Enoch … By faith Noah … By faith Abraham … By faith Jacob … By faith Joseph … By faith Moses … who through faith conquered kingdoms, administered justice, and gained what was promised (Hebrews 11:4–33).

Keep this in mind also: "Without faith it is impossible to please God" (Hebrews 11:6). Those who reject the Christian faith are telling God, "We can get along without You; we don't need your help." With bitter remorse they will someday discover how wrong they were! Also, where Jesus found no faith, there were no mighty deeds: "And [Jesus] did not do many miracles there because of their lack of faith" (Matthew 13:58).

Pray that the Holy Spirit works in you a growing faith. God says, "Build yourselves up in your most holy faith and pray in the Holy Spirit" (Jude 20). Therefore, "Stand firm in the faith" (1 Corinthians 16:13).

Banners of Psalms

Because they are poetry, the psalms in the Bible contain many memorable phrases. Prize and cherish the samples printed here. Use them in your personal letters and greeting cards to friends; share them with your family; and most of all, write them on the tablet of your heart. Use them for a spiritual lift and to offer encouragement and comfort to those in need.

The LORD confides in those who fear Him; He makes His covenant known to them (25:14).

The LORD accepts my prayer (6:9).

The words of the LORD are flawless (12:6).

You, O LORD, keep my lamp burning (18:28).

Blessed are all who take refuge in Him (2:12).

The LORD blesses His people with peace (29:11).

The law of his God is in his heart; his feet do not slip (37:31).

Wash me, and I will be whiter than snow (51:7).

Create in me a pure heart, O God (51:10).

For He will command His angels concerning you to guard you in all your ways (91:11).

The LORD is my light and my salvation (27:1).

You hear, O LORD, the desire of the afflicted (10:17).

My times are in Your hands (31:15).

O LORD, come quickly to help me (40:13).

List my tears on Your scroll (56:8).

Uphold me, and I will be delivered (119:117).

When I awake, I am still with You (139:18).

God is our refuge and strength (46:1).

You have filled my heart with greater joy (4:7).

Let all who take refuge in You be glad (5:11).

You fill me with joy in Your presence (16:11).

Restore to me the joy of Your salvation (51:12).

Worship the LORD with gladness (100:2).

Blessed is the nation whose God is the LORD (33:12).

I will praise You, O LORD, with all my heart (9:1).

How majestic is Your name in all the earth (8:1).

[I will] rejoice in Your salvation (9:14).

Sing to the LORD a new song (96:1).

This is the day the LORD has made; let us rejoice and be glad in it (118:24).

Worship the LORD in the splendor of His holiness (29:2).

I will be glad and rejoice in You (9:2).

Let us shout aloud to the Rock of our salvation (95:1).

The earth is full of His unfailing love (33:5).

My soul will boast in the LORD (34:2).

Let everything that has breath praise the LORD (150:6).

Banners for Daily Living

Here are some more great phrases to learn and to live out each day.

Walking with God will bring us surely to our destination.

If you want to be great, forget self and serve others.

The poorest person in the world is the one whose only interest is money.

God does not promise a calm passage, but a safe landing.

No enemy can do us as much harm as we do ourselves.

Our moments of highest happiness are those when we help someone.

Being filled with the Holy Spirit is being zealous in faith, praise, prayer, and love.

We cannot be saved by works, but we can be lost without them.

He is wise who gives away that which he cannot keep, to gain what he cannot lose.

Leave everything in God's hand, and you will discover God's hand in everything.

With the Spirit working in us, we may talk less and say more.

PART II

Mini Devotions

Let God's Word
strengthen your faith daily.

Go home to your family and tell them how much the Lord has done for you, and how He has had mercy on you. Mark 5:19

As Goes the Home, So Goes the Nation

The most important and influential people in America are the parents who are giving their children a Christian education.

Over and above responding to the daily needs of family life, Christian parents are students of God's Word, which has been given to us in the pages of the Holy Bible. In addition to outlining God's wonderful plan of salvation, the Bible offers us lessons in living life the way God intended. As we read and understand God's Word, we grow in faith.

What will daily Bible study and meditation on God's word do for you and your family?

- Teach you what countless blessings our heavenly Father promises

- Sweeten and enrich the home life

- Provide solutions and help to overcome day-to-day family friction, which can be so harmful

- Assist youth and young adults to hold to Christian ideals and prepare them for the future as husbands, wives, and parents in their own homes

- Help each family member to go out to work, school, office, store, or factory with a God-like attitude (different from the attitude that prevails in today's society)

- Raise a consciousness that God is with you and for you throughout the day as you meet challenges

- Inspire others by your example to make Christ and His church a part of their homes and lives as well

- Give honor and glory to the heavenly Father, expressing gratitude for His daily grace and love

A fuller life for you hinges on three key things: an *initial act*, a *fixed purpose*, and a *daily habit*. The initial act is your resolve to live out your Baptism in Christ Jesus in your daily living as you praise Jesus for His salvation and seek to forgive others. The fixed purpose is to help others discover the many rich blessings of the Christian life. The daily habit is to let God speak through His Word daily through Bible reading and study. If you have not tried this, now is a great time to begin!

Prayer: Holy Spirit, keep me convinced that a Christian home is the greatest school of learning and living. Amen.

Just as sin entered the world through one man,
and death through sin, … death came to all
men, because all sinned. Romans 5:12

How Did Trouble Enter God's Beautiful World?

We know from the Bible that Adam and Eve were the first people to live on the earth. These first parents bore the dignity, beauty, and high intelligence of God's divine image. The divine image is the "new self, created to be like God in true righteousness and holiness" (Ephesians 4:24).

We don't know how long Adam and Eve lived in the state of innocence. We do know that it was Satan who invented sin and brought it into the world. Satan's strategy to ensnare mankind was masterful. He asked them, "Did God really say, 'You must not eat from any tree in the garden'?" Eve, unaware that the question was loaded, answered naively, "We may eat fruit from the trees in the garden but God did say, 'You must not eat fruit from the tree that is in the middle of the garden, and you must not touch it, or you will die.' " (Genesis 3:2–3). Adam and Eve had made up their minds not even to touch the tree.

Satan saw Adam and Eve's determination to be true to God. Only one path was open: he must lead these people to doubt God's word. And this he did, suggesting that God was depriving them of a higher rank. He was very convincing, and our first parents ate the forbidden fruit.

God had warned them, "You will die if you sin." And die they did. No eternity would be spent in the Garden of Eden. God's creative masterpiece, man—pure and holy—and God's beautiful world were ravaged by sin.

But God in His love for the shining star of His creation devised a plan to rescue us from sin, death, and the power of the devil. That plan grabbed the punishment we deserved because of our disobedience and placed it on the sinless Son of God: Jesus. Through Jesus' blood shed on the cross God grants us forgiveness from sin and eternal life.

"For God so loved the world that He gave His one and only Son, that whoever believes in Him shall not perish but have eternal life" (John 3:16).

Prayer: Heavenly Father, keep me aware of my total loss in sin, and my *complete* salvation in Christ. Amen.

Blessed is the man whose sin the Lord will never count against him. Romans 4:8

God Took His Stand on Our Side

God did not reject His fallen children with an icy justice. He chose to take His place at their side. A god (with a lowercase *g*) who allows his children to fall under evil powers and makes no provision for their escape is not the God of the Bible—nor a father, as the Bible describes Him.

Humanity's dilemma seemed hopeless with the fall into sin. People did not have a chance to work their way out of the traps of sin and its curses. Only God could do that—and He did! Do you remember the words from John 3:16? "For God so loved the world that He gave His one and only Son [into punishment], that whoever believes in Him shall not perish but have eternal life." That is an unearned and undeserved gift!

How are we able to walk away confidently from sin in our lives and in our world? This is our confidence: "Because of His great love for us, God, who is rich in mercy, made us alive with Christ even when we were dead in transgressions—it is by grace you have been saved" (Ephesians 2:4–5).

Can we walk confidently into the open, welcoming arms of the redeeming Christ? "God exalted Him to the highest place and gave Him the name that is above every name, that at the name of Jesus every knee should bow, in heaven and on earth and under the earth, and every tongue confess that Jesus Christ is Lord, to the glory of God the Father" (Philippians 2:9–11).

Prayer: Dear Lord, You promised, "By grace [I] have been saved" (Ephesians 2:5). I thank You for this blessed assurance. Amen.

*Delight yourself in the Lord and He will give you
the desires of your heart. Psalm 37:4*

Find Delight in Our Delightful Lord

There is an old Persian proverb that says, "If you have two coins, use one to buy bread for the body and the other to buy a hyacinth for the soul." We need more in life than eating, dressing, making money, paying bills. St. Paul tells us to live "worthy of the Lord," aiming to please Him, "joyfully giving thanks to the Father, who has qualified you to share in the inheritance" (Colossians 1:10–12).

Ask yourself this question: Am I delighted about anything? Ask especially, Am I delighted that I know the Lord? Do I love Him with all my heart? Is He dear to me? Am I glad and happy to have Him as my Savior and my friend?

We can be certain of this: God is delighted in us. His delight in Jesus led His only Son to Calvary, where He suffered and died for our sins. Having satisfied His own demand for justice, God wants us to enjoy contentment in this life, under His care. He wants us to find joy in His grace. He wants us to echo the words of the psalmist, "Oh, how I love Your law! I meditate on it all day long. ... How sweet are Your words to my taste, sweeter than honey to my mouth" (Psalm 119:97, 103).

Read the psalms often. They overflow with the happiness that filled the hearts and minds of those inspired to write them. It seems that they could hardly find words to express their delight, their unbounded joy, their intense happiness in the Lord.

Prayer: Dear Lord, thank You for the abundant life that is mine now and for the eternal life of glory that awaits me through Jesus. Amen.

By this I will know that God is for me.
Psalm 56:9

Is God for Me?

This I know: God is for me. If you can believe that without doubt, you are a very rich person and your heart will be filled with joy. This verse may be one of the least quoted verses in the Bible. Knowing and believing these words, "I know that God is for me," will brighten every day and lighten your every burden.

King David wrote these words on a day when things looked bad for him. There were all kinds of enemies who were out to get him. David thought of the many things that were wrong, and the thought must have terrified him. Then a light blazed through his soul. He said to himself, "Then my enemies will turn back when I call for help. By this I will know that God is for me."

Can you say that, too? Surely you can, because you know that God sent His Son to the cross to prove that He is for us. "God did not send His Son into the world to condemn the world, but to save the world through Him" (John 3:17).

This one thing we must know and cling to: God is for us and He spared not His only begotten Son, but gave Him up for us all. With Him He will freely give us all that we need. That is song and sunshine for our souls!

Prayer: Dear God, show me what a rich person I am, with holy angels all around me, the promise of heaven before me. Thank You for making me so rich. Amen.

We have this hope as an anchor for the soul,
firm and secure. Hebrews 6:19

The Hope of a Golden Future

Hope is a key word in the Bible. Along with faith and love, it is a cardinal Christian virtue. God's Word is resonant with sounds of hope. In it are many assurances of buoyant hope, but no hint of failure.

Hope is faith stretched out. It clings to the promises, for we know they will be fulfilled. Christian hope gives us a forward look. For us the trumpets are sounding on the other shore.

Simon Peter, apostle of hope, urges us, "Set your hope fully on the grace to be given you when Jesus Christ is revealed" (1 Peter 1:13). We can be certain of this: the best is yet to come. We are living on the doorstep of eternal health and happiness. Every step is a step toward triumph and victory. St. Paul exults, "We always thank God ... [because of] the hope that is stored up for you in heaven" (Colossians 1:3, 5). Peter calls it a "living hope ... an inheritance that can never perish, spoil, or fade—kept in heaven for you" (1 Peter 1:3–4).

For every person on earth, life is either a hopeless end or an endless hope. Praise God for His precious gift of hope.

Prayer: O Lord, let the golden hope of a joyful hereafter brighten every moment of my life. Amen.

Do not judge, or you too will be judged. For in the same way you judge others, you will be judged. Matthew 7:1–2

Judging Others Is Bad Business

The humorist Will Rogers had a clever line: "We are all ignorant, only on different subjects." He could have said also, "We all sin, only in different ways." People who sin one way have no right to judge others who sin another way.

Judging others really is bad business. It involves us in deadly consequences. God put it on the line: "You, therefore, have no excuse, you who pass judgment on someone else, for at whatever point you judge the other, you are condemning yourself, because you who pass judgment do the same things" (Romans 2:1).

God knows that we judge others to hurt them and to make ourselves look good. What we are implying is that we never do anything like the others are doing. Perhaps not. But what we do do may be worse. Having once been enlightened by the Holy Spirit, we may in fact be much worse than others, simply because we ought to be much better. Judging others is not only ridiculous, it is just plain stupid. This is what God says: "In the same way you judge others, you will be judged" (Matthew 7:2). By the standard we have set in judging others, God will judge us. We will be getting a dose of our own medicine.

Let us therefore resolve to overcome and avoid all offensive judging. As Jesus forgives us and serves us (who do not deserve it), so we are inspired as Christians to love and to serve others who may not deserve it. Empowered by God's love for us, let this be our resolve—to love more, to judge less.

Prayer: O Holy Spirit, let me always keep in mind that I lose ground when I throw dirt at others. Amen.

Jesus said ... "Go and proclaim
the kingdom of God."
Luke 9:60

Keep the Kingdom First and Foremost

The highest and greatest cause in the world is the cause of God's kingdom. This cause does the most good, helps the most people, is the nearest to the heart of God. Dedication to this cause will make your life rich and meaningful.

In the Lord's Prayer, Jesus taught us to pray, "Thy kingdom come." To advance God's Kingdom is to be our first and foremost aspiration. Nothing is more pleasing to God than to save souls from eternal death. Jesus said, "Seek first His kingdom and His righteousness, and all these things will be given to you as well" (Matthew 6:33).

Early Christian believers walked the glory road of kingdom service. Their zeal grew out of God's great love for them, demonstrated in His Son's death and resurrection. They firmly believed in the positive worth of their mission: to transform human lives through the love of God in Christ.

As one who is earnestly devoted to soul-saving work, follow this daily resolve: I will make every contact with every person a Kingdom contact.

Exhibit these Kingdom virtues in all you do and say: singing faith, joyful praise, radiant hope, loving service.

Prayer: O Holy Spirit, keep the Kingdom first and foremost in my thoughts, in my prayers, in my daily activities, and in my conversations. Amen.

Preserve my life, O LORD, according to Your word. Psalm 119:107

Let the Bible Be Near and Dear to You

Dwight Moody, a great lover of the Bible, gave us these illustrious words about it: "This book contains the mind of God, the state of man, the way of salvation, the doom of sinners, and the happiness of believers. Its doctrines are holy, its precepts are binding, its histories are true, and its decisions are immutable."

Read the Bible in order to be wise, believe it in order to be safe, and practice it in order to be holy. It contains light to direct you, food to support you, and comfort to cheer you. It is the traveler's map, the pilgrim's staff, the pilot's compass, the soldier's sword, and the Christian's charter. Here the gates of hell are revealed, paradise is restored, and heaven is opened.

Christ is its grand subject, our good its design, and the glory of God its end. It should fill the memory, rule the heart, and guide the feet. Read it slowly, frequently and prayerfully. If you are a first timer, find a friendly Bible study group with a knowledgeable leader, or purchase a "one-year" Bible that will guide you through an illuminating "first walk" through God's Word.

The Bible is a gold mine filled with treasures, given to you throughout your lifetime. It will be opened at the judgment, and be remembered forever. It involves the highest responsibility, will reward the greatest labor, and condemn all who trifle with its sacred contents.

Prayer: O Holy Spirit, help me to love, honor, and follow the Bible. Amen.

And now these three remain: faith, hope and
love. But the greatest of these is love.
1 Corinthians 13:13

Put Love First in Your Life

Faith brings us to God; love makes us to be like God. The faith that loves is the faith that saves. "The only thing that counts is faith expressing itself through love" (Galatians 5:6).

The early believers walked the glory road of loving service to mankind. Motivated by God's love in Christ Jesus, this is what they said: "Let us love one another" (1 John 4:7). All who observed those early Christians commented, "See how they love one another!"

God puts it on the line: "Be devoted to one another in brotherly love. Honor one another above yourselves" (Romans 12:10); "Serve one another in love" (Galatians 5:13); "The fruit of the Spirit is love" (Galatians 5:22).

What should be our resolve? That empowered by God's love revealed to us in Jesus, we will make every contact with every person a love contact. Here is a recommendation from Henry Drummond, author of "The Greatest Thing in the World," which for years, next to the Bible, was the most read book in America: "Let every Christian read First Corinthians chapter 13 (known as the "love" chapter) every day for three weeks. Your life will be transformed." One person who followed this advice stated, "I never started living until I started loving."

Prayer: O Holy Spirit, fill my soul with the spirit of Your love—love first revealed in the person and work of Jesus; then my attitude will show true altitude. Amen.

[Jesus said,] "Because you have so little faith
I tell you the truth, if you have faith
as small as a mustard seed, …
nothing will be impossible for you."
Matthew 17:20

Strong Faith + Fervent Prayer = A Dynamic Combination

Jesus used an incident in the lives of His disciples to teach them this lesson: Strong faith and fervent prayer go together.

While Jesus was away, a desperate father brought his epileptic son to the disciples for healing. The disciples tried, but failed to heal him. When Jesus returned He was a bit irritated with them. He said, "How long shall I put up with you?" He then proceeded to heal the boy.

Of course, later the disciples wanted to know why they were unable to do the job. Jesus explained, "This kind [of demon] does not go out except by prayer and fasting" (Matthew 17:21). He told them they could have healed the boy had they only removed every hindrance and given themselves to fervent prayer.

There is a lesson here for all of us. If we are really in trouble, we must devote ourselves to prayer. Remember the invitation of our Savior: "Come to Me, all you who are weary and burdened, and I will give you rest (Matthew 11:28).

Prayer: O Holy Spirit, remind me of my Savior's invitation: that coming to Him in prayer is the best way to solve big problems. Amen.

[All who believe] are justified freely by His grace
through the redemption that came
by Christ Jesus.
Romans 3:24

The Heart and Center of Our Faith

The supreme question of your life may just be "How can a person get into a right relationship with God?" As big as that question may seem, God gives us a crystal clear answer. We are justified freely and fully by His grace, through the ransom that Jesus Christ paid for us on the cross. To make sure that you understand this, let's put it this way: God justifies sinners by a gift of grace, through faith in Jesus Christ, with no need for our own good deeds to accomplish this.

Two things happen when we are justified: Our sins against God's Law are forgiven, and Christ's fulfillment of the Law is credited to our account.

When God makes the pronouncement "Not Guilty" on a person who is guilty, He appears to be in violation of justice. The opposite is true. The only just ground on which God pardons and accepts a sinner is that Jesus Christ paid our debt of sin in full through His death on the cross. "The LORD has laid on Him the iniquity of us all" (Isaiah 53:6). If our justification depended upon a courtroom trial and a jury of our peers, we'd all be lost.

It seems too good to be true, but it is true, just as God's Word is true. We can believe from the heart that we are fully justified, fully forgiven through the merit of Jesus Christ our Lord. We can shout with Paul, "If God is for us, who can be against us?" (Romans 8:31).

Prayer: Thank You, Lord Jesus, for paying my sin-debt in full. Amen.

Fan into flame the gift of God, which is in you.
2 Timothy 1:6

Use the Power You Already Have

Just think of the great source of power there is going on inside of us and every other believer in Christ: The same power that raised Jesus Christ from the dead. St. Paul explains that "God did not give us a spirit of timidity, but a spirit of power, of love and of self-discipline" (2 Timothy 1:7).

This is Jesus' promise to His believing children: "You will receive power when the Holy Spirit comes on you; and you will be My witnesses" (Acts 1:8). Every Christian is a "power station" linked with Jesus, who said, "All authority in heaven and on earth has been given to Me" (Matthew 28:18). Therefore, undertake a great mission for God and walk with Him.

Think of what would happen if every Christian would bravely, in faith and confidence, express this power in prayer and witnessing! With this power working in us, we can undertake great projects for God and expect the great blessings He promised.

With kind words on our lips and good will in our hearts, we can bestow warmth and cheer on everyone we meet in this cold world.

Prayer: O Holy Spirit, strengthen my faith through God's Word, so that I may boldly proclaim Your promised power. Amen.

[God] gave Him the name that is above every
name, that at the name of Jesus every knee
should bow, in heaven and on earth and under
the earth, and every tongue confess that Jesus
Christ is Lord, to the glory of God the Father.
Philippians 2:9–11

Use the Mighty Name of Jesus

A newspaper article told of an 18-year-old girl, working as a clerk in a drugstore, who was ordered by a holdup man, "Put all the money in a bag or lose your life." She pleaded with him, "In Jesus' name, don't take this money." Amazed and amused, the robber asked, "What did you say?" The girl answered, "Jesus has something much better for you; please don't take this money." There was an unbelievable change inside the holdup man. "Thank you," he said, and he left.

Was it the girl's cool that baffled the robber, or was it the power of Jesus' name? Either way, there is power in Jesus' name. The devil flinches when a believer takes authority over a bad situation in the mighty name of Jesus. Just mention His all-powerful name. He will always help those who come to Him for help. The authority of His name is available to us in every situation. That doesn't mean every robbery will be stopped, but it does mean that any supposed "victory" by Satan is only temporary. God has already vanquished the evil one.

Jesus was always speaking words like "Fear not, only believe," "I am with you!" and "I will help you." Through God's Word the Holy Spirit will strengthen our faith in Jesus, our Savior. Faith in Him will enable us to win the victory over life's problems. All day and every day we can be sure that He is with us, ready to help.

Prayer: Dear Jesus, I know that if I turn to You I will always be on victorious ground. Amen.

The King [Jesus] will reply, "I tell you the truth,
whatever you did for one of the least of these
brothers of Mine, you did for Me."
Matthew 25:40

Do Everything as If It Were for Jesus

In his poem "The Shoes of Happiness," Edwin Markham tells of Conrad the cobbler, who dreamed one night that Jesus would come to be his guest. When the dawn broke, he rose and decorated his little shop with bright flowers and then waited. When the Master would come, the cobbler planned to wash His feet where the spikes had been and kiss the hands where the nails went in. But the Master did not come.

A poor traveler entered his shop, and Conrad gave him a pair of shoes. An old woman came bent from the weight of a heavy burden. Conrad lifted the load off her back and refreshed her with food. Finally, just before sunset, a lost little girl came. Her eyes were wet with tears and in pity Conrad led her back to her mother. But the divine guest never came. Then soft in the silence he heard a voice, "Lift up your heart, for I kept My word. Three times I came to your friendly door; three times My shadow was on your floor. I was the beggar with bruised feet. I was the woman you gave food to eat. I was the child you brought back to her mother."

Prayer: Dear Jesus, inspire me to do something beautiful and true for those in need, knowing that I am doing it for You. Amen.

*[Jesus said,] "I will see you again and you will
rejoice, and no one will take away your joy."*
John 16:22

Joy beyond All Telling

The Christian life is a life of joy. Jesus, though "a
man of sorrows and acquainted with grief," was the
most joy-filled person who ever walked this earth. In
the darkest night of His life He prayed as He prepared
to die for the sins of all people. His prayer: that His disciples might feel His complete joy in their hearts.

When you are young, thoughts of sorrow and suffering are sometimes the farthest from your mind. If
you have been fortunate in this life to be spared any
sorrow thus far, it is a rare thing indeed. Pain, though,
will enter your life sometime. In heaven, however, all
earthly sorrow and suffering is turned into heavenly
song and sunshine. Bitter teardrops turn into glistening
diamonds of joy. "Those who sow in tears will reap
with songs of joy. He who goes out weeping, ... will
return with songs of joy" (Psalm 126:5–6). This is our
Lord's promise: "The ransomed of the Lord will return.
They will enter Zion with singing; everlasting joy will
crown their heads. Gladness and joy will overtake
them, and sorrow and sighing will flee away" (Isaiah
35:10).

St. Paul, author of the epistle of joy (Philippians),
has this advice: "Rejoice in the Lord always. I will say it
again: Rejoice!" (Philippians 4:4). And that we do, for

our names are written in heaven (Luke 10:20). "With joy you will draw water from the wells of salvation" (Isaiah 12:3).

Prayer: Dear Jesus, I know that You would like me to have Your joy, and I certainly would enjoy having it. Amen.

[Jesus said:] *"Surely I am with you always, to*
the very end of the age." Matthew 28:20

Enjoy Living with Jesus in Your Life

Think this through and believe it from the heart: Jesus Christ, the Son of God and Redeemer of the world, the King of kings and Lord of lords, is always with us. How rich we are in that promise!

He is with us here and now. He is with us on the freeway. He is with us in our homes. He is with us in our leisure hours. He is with us in good days and bad days, in health and sickness, in prosperity or adversity, in life and death.

This is not just a wish or a hope. It is a promise, reliable and unshakable, fully true, coming from Him who said, "I am the way and the truth and the life" (John 14:6).

Cherish this promise, for it puts your feet on solid ground. It lifts your life to the highest level. We have the best friend in the world to walk with and talk with. We are in the best and safest company. When problems and enemies attack us, let us remember that they must also attack Him who is with us and for us.

Prayer: O Holy Spirit, every day and every step of the way, please remind me that Jesus walks with me. Amen.

The LORD is my shepherd, I shall not be in want.
Psalm 23:1

I Am a Sheep Who Needs a Shepherd

Psalm 23 is a well-known gem. You may have it memorized. If so, you know the way it brings great comfort, contentment, and peace.

A little girl returning from Sunday school said excitedly to her mother, "Mother, we are learning the twenty-third psalm, and I already know the first verse."

"That's fine, said her mom. "And what is the first verse?"

The little girl didn't remember it perfectly, but her theology was right on the mark: "The Lord is my shepherd, that's all I want."

Because He truly is your shepherd, you can be confident that He will take care of you. He is a good Shepherd who will truly care for the sheep of His flock. In John's gospel Jesus reminds us that He is the Good Shepherd who "lays down His life for the sheep" (John 10:11). He is not a hireling who flees when he sees the wolf coming. We are members of His flock; we belong to Him, and He will take care of us no matter how difficult the task may be.

Prayer: O Holy Spirit, help us to keep on saying and believing, "The LORD is my shepherd, I shall not be in want." Amen.

In Him [Jesus] … we have the forgiveness of
sins, in accordance with the riches
of God's grace. Ephesians 1:7

What Is Our Greatest Problem?

Most every thinking person will agree that sin is our greatest problem. How fortunate we are that God made it His problem too! How did He handle it? "God was reconciling the world to Himself in Christ, not counting men's sins against them. … God made Him who had no sin to be sin for us, so that in Him we might become the righteousness of God" (2 Corinthians 5:19, 21). Sin is the reason for the writing of the Bible; grace is its content.

Because He loves us, God wants us to do several things:

Confess our sins. "If we confess our sins, He is faithful and just and will forgive us our sins" (1 John 1:9).

Receive His forgiveness. "Your sins have been forgiven on account of His name" (1 John 2:12).

Believe that our sins are forever removed. "As far as the east is from the west, so far has He removed our transgressions from us" (Psalm 103:12).

Believe that as God forgets our sins, so should we. "Their sins and lawless acts I will remember no more" (Hebrews 10:17).

Thank, praise, and glorify God without ceasing for doing all this for us.

Prayer: Thousand, thousand thanks shall be, dearest Jesus, unto Thee. Amen.

Dear friend, I pray that you may enjoy good
health and that all may go well with you.
3 John 2

God Wants You to Be Healthy and Happy

If your body could talk to you, what would it say? "You are really giving me a rough time; you are full of hostility, hate, fear, doubt, despair, self-pity, malice and envy—in short, you make me sick!" Or would it say, "You are so full of good will, love, tolerance, generosity, you make it easy for me to live with you; together we make a great team!"

Nothing contributes so much to health as a constant flow of happiness. Contentment under God's care, joy in His grace, and caring love for others are powerful ingredients toward spiritual and physical well-being.

The happiness God gives comes from the joy of knowing that He has provided us eternal life through Jesus. Jesus suggested that our innermost being may be compared to drinking from an artesian well: "Whoever drinks the water I give him will never thirst" (John 4:14).

The key to happiness is to know God as our Father, Christ as our Savior, and the Holy Spirit as our companion and guide. God's arms hold us up, the Holy Spirit lives within us, and the angels watch over us. The glory of heaven is before us. We can be happy with the Lord by our side.

Prayer: O Holy Spirit, give me the wisdom to pursue all that is godly and true, holy and sincere, as I trust in Jesus' endless love, so that I may be healthy and happy. Amen.

For the joy set before Him [Jesus] endured the cross, scorning its shame, and sat down at the right hand of the throne of God.
Hebrews 12:2

Here's Something You Should Not Forget

When your turn comes to endure some trial, don't think that God is using cruel and unjust therapy on you. God has these reassuring words for you: "Dear friends, do not be surprised at the painful trial you are suffering, as though something strange were happening to you. But rejoice that you participate in the sufferings of Christ, so that you may be overjoyed when His glory is revealed" (1 Peter 4:12–13).

Remember this: Christ's suffering was the gateway to His glory. He drank the bitter cup that led to victory. The hands that were crushed by the cruel hammer blow now hold the scepter of power and dominion. Those nail-bruised feet of His now have ascended to a throne. His thorn-crowned head now bears a kingly crown of glory. Whatever draws us closer to God—no matter how difficult it is to bear at the moment—will turn out to be a hidden blessing for which we will be eternally thankful. The best days of our lives are those when we have God foremost in our thoughts and are driven to His Word, deepening our love for Him, strengthening our faith, and raising our hopes.

Prayer: Dear God, make me forever thankful that You lead me through the trials I may encounter. Amen.

The greatest among you will be your servant. For whoever exalts himself will be humbled, and whoever humbles himself will be exalted.
Matthew 23:11–12

The More You Serve, the Better You Feel

When Jesus walked this earth, He didn't act like a dictator or a ruler, but as a humble servant. Mount Calvary, His dying on the cross, was His greatest and final act of servanthood. The Bible says of Him, "The Son of Man [Jesus] did not come to be served, but to serve" (Mark 10:45).

Jesus taught clearly that we should think of ourselves as servants. Not a popular or familiar idea in today's society of "get anything you want, and fast!" For us to serve rather than be served is a rather foreign concept. The New Testament cajoles us— "I will show you my faith by what I do" (James 2:18). Jesus Christ is our "service station." It's to Him we go when we need to be "refueled" for service. God has given us so much to share with others! Motivated by the Jesus who came to serve us, we can embrace the famous words of St. Francis:

Lord, make me an instrument of Your peace.
Where there is hatred, let me sow love;
where there is injury, pardon;
where there is discord, union;
where there is doubt, faith;
where there is despair, hope;

where there is darkness, light;
where there is sadness, joy.
Oh, divine Master, grant that I may not so much
seek
to be consoled as to console;
to be understood as to understand;
to be loved as to love.
For it is in giving that we receive;
it is in pardoning that we are pardoned;
it is in dying that we are born to eternal life.

Prayer: Dear Lord, help me to have the same attitude and humility as Jesus had for serving others. Amen.

Let your light shine before men, that they may
see your good deeds
and praise your Father in heaven.
Matthew 5:16

Be a Good Samaritan

The tale of the Good Samaritan (Luke 10:25–37) introduces us to three different mind sets:

The robber: "What's yours is mine; I'll take it."

Priest and Levite: "What's mine is mine; I'll keep it."

Good Samaritan: "What's mine is yours; let's share it."

Jesus' love for us motivates us to go and do as the Samaritan did.

The Bible says, "Therefore, as we have opportunity, let us do good to all people, especially to those who belong to the family of believers" (Galatians: 6:10). That we have the wherewithal to do good is obvious, as we take stock of all God has given us. "The eyes of all look to You, and You give them their food at the proper time. You open Your hand and satisfy the desires of every living thing" (Psalm 145:15–16). We thank God for His blessings, and we use them according to His direction.

Concerning us who have received great blessings, Jesus said, "From the one who has been entrusted with much, much more will be asked" (Luke 12:48). We certainly have been given much through our relationship with the Lord Jesus Christ. We in turn reflect His love with lives filled with faith, joy, praise, loving service, and generosity.

Prayer: Dear Lord, teach me how to be a faithful servant and manager of all Your gifts. Amen.

This is my prayer that your love may abound
more and more in knowledge
and depth of insight.
Philippians 1:9

Exhibit Genuine, Overflowing Love

There is no joy like the joy of living in love. Without love, life is one big emptiness. Someone who is loveless can cause more rifts and hurt more feelings than the someone who never darkened the door of a church. Using a loveless "Christian" as the destructive instrument, the devil can undermine ministry efforts in the most subtle ways.

Our churches of today would be filled to overflowing if people were sure that they would find love there. Nothing will make the Christian cause more attractive than love in action. A living sermon of love is our most effective witness to the living Lord of love.

Early Christians were conspicuous because of their love. They believed in doing and showing love to mankind through service. (It's that "servant" thing again!) Their vigor and zeal grew out of their faith in the worth of their mission to transform the world through the love of God in Christ Jesus.

Through faith in Jesus, love is our most visible virtue. Jesus directs, "As the Father has loved Me, so have I loved you. Now remain in My love. If you obey My commands, you will remain in My love, just as I have obeyed My Father's commands and remain in His love" (John 15:9–10). Actually, that's not as much a command as it is a description of those who have been filled with Jesus' love for them—filled to overflowing.

Prayer: Lord of love, fill my heart with love. Amen.

Everyone who believes in Him receives forgive-
ness of sins through His name. Acts 10:43

God's Love and Forgiveness
Go Out to His Children

God clearly laid down this principle: The Bible was written because of sin; but grace is its essential content. When we realize that we are totally lost in sin, we will find great joy in our complete redemption through Christ.

The Bible is a long book. It isn't like a novel that you can complete in a few days of reading. It takes many hours to read—possibly even weeks, months, or years! But its basic content can be reduced to just a few words: sin and grace, Law and Gospel (Good News). The Law is an SOS: it shows our sins. The Gospel is also an SOS: it shows our Savior.

God's creative masterpieces, man and the world, once pure and holy, were ravaged by sin. "Every inclination of the thoughts of [peoples'] heart was only evil all the time" (Genesis 6:5).

Jesus diagnosed the human heart this way: "What comes out of a man is what makes him 'unclean.' For from within, out of men's hearts, come evil thoughts, sexual immorality, theft, murder, adultery, greed, malice, deceit, lewdness, envy, slander, arrogance and folly. All these evils come from inside and make a man 'unclean' " (Mark 7:20–23).

We may resent and reject this assessment of our heart's status, but history and human experience have proven it to be true. Just read the daily newspaper!

St. Paul reminds us of our rescue: "As for you, you were dead in your transgressions and sins. … But because of His great love for us, God, who is rich in mercy, made us alive with Christ even when we were dead in transgressions—it is by grace you have been saved … and this not from yourselves, it is the gift of God" (Ephesians 2:1, 4–5, 8).

Prayer: O Holy Spirit, enable me through faith to confess that my redemption is complete through Christ, the hope of glory. Amen.

Let the weakling say, "I am strong." Joel 3:10

How Do the Weak Become Strong?

In the poem "Invictus," by William Henley, there is a much-quoted line: "I am the master of my fate; I am the captain of my soul." These are brash and boastful words that deny the teachings of Christ. But when death took Henley's six-year-old daughter, his bravado melted. He discovered that we are not masters of our fate nor captains of our souls.

A hymn stanza says, "We are weak and heavy-laden, cumbered with a load of care." True that is. However, we also confess that God is strong. St. Paul wrote, "For when I am weak," that is, when I am not trying to save myself, "then am I strong," that is, God's strength shows through (2 Corinthians 12:10). In his weakness Paul discovered the Lord's sustaining grace and strength.

David had it right: "The LORD is my strength and my shield; my heart trusts in Him, and I am helped" (Psalm 28:7).

The prophet Isaiah declared: "Those who hope in the LORD will renew their strength" (Isaiah 40:31). With Paul we can affirm: "I can do everything through Him who gives me strength" (Philippians 4:13). "My grace is sufficient for you, for My power is made perfect in weakness" (2 Corinthians 12:9).

Not I, then, but Christ my Savior is the Master of my life, the Captain of my soul. He makes the weak strong.

Prayer: Lord Jesus, I am counting on You to keep me strong in faith, in love, and in serving You. Amen.

The unfading beauty of a gentle and quiet spirit
… is of great worth in God's sight. 1 Peter 3:4

Would You Like to Be Beautiful?

A Christian woman was asked about the secret of her beauty. She said, "For my lips I use truth, for my voice I use prayer, for my eyes I use pity, for my hands I use charity, for my figure I use uprightness, for my heart I use love."

We are all concerned about our outer appearance. Advertising just won't let us forget. But God is concerned about our *inner* beauty, and He gives us the recipe for it. God doesn't object to respectable and attractive adornment of the body, but He tells us that there is something much better than well-dressed outward beauty: it is the inward beauty of a meek and quiet spirit.

If you want to be a beautiful person, you must have a beautiful spirit. What makes us beautiful in God's sight is faith in the Savior; joy in the promises of God; God's peace ruling within us; His Spirit filling us with kindness, love, meekness, self-control, and uprightness.

Prayer: Dear Lord, keep me well dressed in the beauty of faith and holiness. Amen.

The Lord disciplines those He loves.
Hebrews 12:6

Why Does God Discipline Those Whom He Loves?

When visiting a good friend in the hospital, a pastor said, "George, remember: whom the Lord loves, He disciplines." The friend answered, "If that's the case, I wish He wouldn't love me so much."

Sometimes life hurls us into a frenzy of distress. We may ask, "O, Lord, what are You doing to me?" At such times we should know that God has something in mind for us, something involving our good. He allows trials to come, so that we may be drawn closer to Him.

Think of the black and white keys on a piano. Both are necessary for beautiful music. Likewise, bright and dark days, joys and sorrows are needed to keep us in humility, in repentance, and in readiness for Christ's return.

When there is trouble, we go to God for help. When we go to God for help, we always receive it. Through faith, strengthened by the Holy Spirit, working through God's Word we can echo the words of St. Paul, "In all these things we are more than conquerors. … I am convinced that … neither the present nor the future … will be able to separate us from the love of God that is in Christ Jesus our Lord" (Romans 8:37–39).

Prayer: Dear Lord, for sunny days and dark days we give You praise. Amen.

Above all else, guard your heart, for it is the wellspring of life. Proverbs 4:23

Good Heart-Keeping Is like Good House-Keeping

Good housekeeping is important. Good heart-keeping is more important.

In a way, our hearts are similar to our homes. They have a way of becoming cluttered and littered with all kinds of things. Our hearts, as our homes, may become places of disorder and confusion.

A well-kept heart is rooted in God and in His Word. Through faith, strengthened by God's Word, we give thanks that salvation is ours through the Lord Jesus Christ.

God says, "Seek first His kingdom and His righteousness, and all these things will be given to you as well" (Matthew 6:33). It is very important physically to have a good heart. It is more important spiritually to have a good heart. Hudson Taylor lived a wonderful life of trust. Here is what he said: "Let us give up our work, our thoughts, our plans, ourselves, our lives, our loved ones, into His hands. When we have given all unto God, there will be nothing left for us to worry about."

Prayer: Dear Lord Jesus, continue to do Your work in me and through me. Amen.

But the Counselor, the Holy Spirit … will teach you all things and will remind you of everything I have said to you. John 14:26–27

The Greatest Teacher in the World

What the Holy Spirit did for Simeon, a godly, lovable member of the Kingdom, He has done for us. The aged Simeon wanted above all to see the Christ child before he himself died. He asked the Holy Spirit to make this possible. And He did. He led Simeon into the temple when Joseph and Mary brought in the Child. Jubilantly, Simeon took the Child in his arms and said, "[Lord,] You now dismiss Your servant in peace. For my eyes have seen Your salvation" (Luke 2:28).

The Word of God says "Ask … seek … knock" (Matthew 7:7). That's what Simeon did, and the Holy Spirit granted his prayer.

We can learn much here. The Holy Spirit has already done something great for us. He has revealed our sin *and* our complete redemption in Christ. He continues to do His work in us as we study, read, and share God's Word. He fills us with great zeal to live a life of peace.

Prayer: Holy Spirit, enter in, and in my heart Your work begin. Amen.

The Lord Jesus Christ ... will transform our lowly
bodies so that they will be like His glorious body.
Philippians 3:20–21

Beautiful Bodies in a Beautiful World

Our earthly bodies are vulnerable to disease, disfigurement, and death. On the average, we're supposed to last about three score years and ten (70). Then we'll wear out, grow faint, and approach death. In contrast, our redeemed and resurrected bodies will be vigorous, beautiful, hale and hearty, suited for life in the new world.

This is what the Bible says: "The Lord Himself will come down from heaven, with a loud command, ... and the dead in Christ will rise first. After that, we who are still alive and left will be caught up together with them in the clouds to meet the Lord in the air. And so we will be the Lord forever" (1 Thessalonians 4:16–17).

The early Christians viewed death as sleep. Thus they named their graveyards *kiometerion*, from which comes the word "cemetery." They were saying in effect that they were putting the dead in a motel, for a little while.

For today's Christians, death is a sunrise, not a sunset; the beginning, not the end. God has made death glorious and triumphant, for through its portals we enter into the presence of Jesus, who loved us and gave His life for us.

Prayer: Dear Lord, help me to believe that every step in my life is a step toward home. Amen.

Though He slay me, yet will I hope in Him.
Job 13:15

Never, Never Doubt God

Do you know the highest compliment we can pay God? It is to trust Him—under *all* circumstances. It's easy to trust God when everything is going right. But to trust Him when everything seems to be going wrong, that shows real faith.

Ancient Job had that kind of faith. After his dreadful ordeal with painful afflictions of soul and body, he said, "Though He slay me, yet will I hope in Him."

Christians may delete from their dictionary such words as luck, fate, and accident. It is simply not true that at any time, a black cat crossing our path means trouble. Or that the stars affect our lives for good or evil. Or that a crystal worn on a chain around our neck is anything more than a pretty rock. Fatalism and the Christian faith cannot live in the same heart. They don't go together; one excludes the other.

As a Christian I can say with total assurance, "As Job did, so I too face the hazards of life; but I know that nothing can strike me apart from God's good and gracious plan for me. The God who loves me so much that He gave His only Son for my salvation will take care of me. Even on the shadowed path He lets me find some lovely flowers that grow only in the shade. 'Surely goodness and love will follow me all the days of my life' " (Psalm 23:6).

Prayer: Dear Jesus, when the path is dark and frightening, help me to believe that You are with me. Amen.

*Whatever you do, whether in word or deed, do it
all in the name of the Lord Jesus.*
Colossians 3:17

For Amazing Results, Follow these Steps

Live these resolutions:

1. Confess Jesus as your Savior—Jesus, who suffered and died on the cross so that you might have life.

2. Understand the difference between a professing and a practicing Christian and strive to be both.

3. Relate your Christian faith to each and every part of your life: work, sports, food, drink, fun, budget.

4. Have a strong prayer life in order to draw God's blessings down upon many people and causes.

5. Exhibit a deep love for your church: attend it to hear God's Word, to receive Holy Communion, and to glorify God's name.

6. Invest your talents in a life of Christian service, and you will feel better and look better.

7. Freely express your love of God and love of others.

8. Live on the sunny side of life, with the Lord Jesus as your manager and guide.

9. Keep in mind what Jesus said: "Apart from Me you can do nothing" (John 15:5). Undertake everything with Him and for Him.

10. Be joyful as you show that yours is a religion of joy.

Prayer: "Praise the LORD, O my soul; and all my inmost being, praise His holy name" (Psalm 103:1). Amen.

*Far be it from me that I should sin against the
LORD by failing to pray for you. 1 Samuel 12:23*

Enrich Your Life by Praying

There are so many things to pray for, yet we forget to do even that. Improve your prayer life by using your hand as a guide.

Your *thumb* is always nearest to you. It suggests that we pray for those near and dear to us: father, mother, brother, sister, relatives, and friends.

Your *index finger* is the teacher's finger. It reminds us to pray for the teachers of the land, that God may give them true love for the children.

The *tall finger* reminds us to pray for the important people in life: the president, high officials, leaders.

The *ring finger,* not as strong as the others, reminds us to pray for the weak and heavy laden, those who are burdened, deprived, depressed.

The *little finger* reminds us to pray for ourselves, for we are to be little in our own eyes.

The God who loved us so much that He willingly sent His only Son to suffer and die for us assures us that He will accomplish wonders in our lives. Since our prayers have such great influence and do so much good, we can aspire to be far-reaching prayer servants who will in our prayers include many people and many causes in many parts of the world.

Prayer: Dear Lord, guide me to be a rich and far-reaching prayer servant. Amen.

*I tell you the truth, My Father will give you
whatever you ask in My name. John 16:23*

Do Your Best Work through Prayer

The Bible speaks of four forms of prayer. God encourages us to exercise all of these opportunities as we live out our faith in Jesus.

Pray privately: Jesus said, "When you pray, go into your room, close the door and pray to your Father" (Matthew 6:6).

Pray together with people: "If two of you on earth agree about anything you ask for, it will done for you by My Father in heaven" (Matthew 18:19). The emphasis here is not on two people praying together, but on their agreement on what they pray for.

Pray with small groups: "Where two or three come together in My name, there am I with them" (Matthew 18:20). When Christians come together, they have great opportunity to achieve mighty blessings through prayer.

Pray with your congregation: After Christ's ascension, the 120 Christians, including Jesus' mother, all kept praying together (Acts 1:14). That may have been the most powerful prayer group ever assembled.

Prayer: O Holy Spirit, through faith enable us to see what a privilege it is to carry everything to God in prayer. Amen.

Faith is being sure of the what we hope for and certain of what we do not see. Hebrews 11:1

Faith Can Accomplish Wonders

Jesus said, "If you have faith as small as a mustard seed, ... nothing will be impossible for you" (Matthew 17:20). That's quite a promise! Is it true? Every promise of God is true. God wants us to live out our faith. It will prove God's wonders. We need only look at one chapter of the Bible: Matthew 9.

Faith Proof 1: The man whose daughter was dying believed that Jesus could help; so he said to Jesus, "Come and put Your hand on her, and she will live" (verse 18). Jesus did, the girl lived (verse 25).

Faith Proof 2: One woman believed that a simple act like touching Jesus' garment in faith would help. Jesus turned to her and said, "Take heart, daughter, ... your faith has healed you" (verse 22).

Faith Proof 3: Jesus asked two blind men, "Do you believe that I am able to do this [that is, heal you]?" They said, "Yes, Lord." Jesus said to them, "According to your faith will it be done to you." And they were healed (verses 27–30).

Faith is the key to the solution of any problem. God provides us the means through which the Holy Spirit works to strengthen our faith in Jesus our Savior: God's Word and the Lord's Supper. If faith can't do it, nothing can. Jesus said, "Don't be afraid; just believe" (Luke 8:50).

Prayer: Dear Jesus, help me by Your Spirit's power to have faith that embraces the fact that Your power is greater than any problem I may have. Amen.

For the joy set before Him [Jesus] endured the
cross, scorning its shame, and sat down at the
right hand of the throne of God.
Hebrews 12:2

True Love Always Finds a Way

Madame Chiang Kai-Shek has shared a tale that shows that true love always finds a way. A Chinese peasant was working on his hilltop farm. Suddenly he felt the earth shaking. He saw the ocean receding far from the shore, getting set for what he knew would be a disruptive tidal wave. His neighbors were working below in the fields, which would soon be flooded. With a torch he set fire to his rice barn and sounded the fire gong. His friends ran up the hill to help him. Then they saw in horror the water covering the fields they had just left behind. They knew what their benefactor had done. The monument they erected in his honor bore these words: "He gave us all he had, and gave it gladly."

Jesus Christ gave us all He had, and gave it gladly. For the joy of having us forever at His side He gave up His life and endured a heavy cross.

We may have no barn to burn, but we do have a love to give. This love we give gladly in gratitude to our great benefactor, who gave us all He had that we might have all we need for this life and the next.

Prayer: Dear Jesus, You endured the dreadful punishment that should have fallen upon us. For this we praise and thank You now and forever. Amen.

Fathers [and mothers] ... bring them [your children] up in the training and instruction of the Lord. Ephesians 6:4

Let Christ Be at Home in Your Home

Let Christ be the head of your home, the silent listener to every conversation, the unseen guest at every meal. This will make your earthly home the greatest school of Christian learning and living. No other factor or place in life determines our future as much as does the home.

The highly honored soprano Madame Schumann-Heink gave us this description of home: "It is the laugh of a baby, the song of a mother, the strength of a father, warmth of loving hearts, light from happy eyes, kindness, loyalty, comradeship. Home is the first school and the first church for the young one, where they learn what is right, what is good, and what is kind. Home is the place where the children find comfort when they are hurt or sick, where their joys are shared, and where their sorrows are eased. Here father and mother are respected and loved. Here children are wanted. Here the simplest food is good enough for kings. In such a home money is not so important as loving kindness. Here even the tea kettle sings for happiness. That is a home—God bless it!"

Remember the story of Zacchaeus? Jesus said to him, "I must stay at your house today" (Luke 19:5). He did, and the man's life was transformed.

Through faith Jesus lives in our hearts and dwells in our home, offering to us His love and forgiveness. Through God's Word the Holy Spirit strengthens our faith, enabling us to have homes where Christ is at home.

Prayer: Dear Jesus, enter Thou my home with me, until I enter Thine with Thee. Amen.

Be wise about what is good, and innocent about what is evil. Romans 16:19

Thank God for Education

Give glory to our great and gracious Lord for instructing us in the branches of Christian learning:

In biology we go back to the very origin of life itself. "In the beginning God created the heavens and the earth" (Genesis 1:1).

In mathematics we know the breadth, length, depth, and height of the love of Christ (Ephesians 3:18).

In theology we stand firmly on the Rock of Ages (Deuteronomy 32:4).

In sociology we have the one and only remedy for sin: the grace of our Lord Jesus Christ (1 John 1:7).

In botany we have discovered the true Vine (John 15:1).

In astronomy we looking toward the bright Morning Star (Revelations 22:16).

In anatomy we know that the heart is deceitful and, by itself, is beyond cure (Jeremiah 17:9)—in need of a transplant that only Jesus' love can provide.

In architecture we can build our lives on the foundation of the chief cornerstone, Jesus Himself (Ephesians 2:20).

Prayer: Dear Jesus, I praise You for revealing to me that the way to heaven is through You, for You said, "I am the Way." Amen.

I will be glad and rejoice in Your love.
Psalm 31:7

Hallelujah! I Am a Christian!

The Christian religion is a religion of joy. It has tons of triumphs and victories, not an ounce of defeat. Jesus said, "No one will take away your joy" (John 16:22).

Just take a look at life as it is; the very opposite seems to be true. People are joyless, discouraged, bored, burdened. We live in a world full of tensions, riots, lawlessness, drugs, drink, sickness, pain. Even young people, who should be living in the fullness of life's joys, are asking, "What's the sense of it all?"

Jesus' answer would be, "I have come to give you life. Receive Me and My way, and you will know the secret of the abundant life."

What is His way? It is the way of

Faith. "He who believes [in Me] has everlasting life" (John 6:47).

Love: "Everyone who loves has been born of God … because God is love" (1 John 4:7–8).

Peace: "My peace I give to you" (John 14:27).

Hope: "Do not let your hearts be troubled. … In My Father's house are many rooms. … I am going there to prepare a place for you" (John 14:1–3).

Prayer: Lord Jesus, give me contentment in Your care, joy in Your grace, zeal for Your cause, and thanksgiving for Your love. Amen.

Blessed are the poor in spirit, for theirs is the kingdom of heaven. Matthew 5:3

Pride Is Really Wrong

What does it mean to be "poor in spirit"? It is the very opposite of being proud. Pride is a primary sin. Pride begets most other sins.

Take the sin of envy. Envy too is pride, for by it we show that we don't think anyone should rise above us.

Anger is self-love. It is pride exhibited in resentment against those who get in our way.

Avarice, greed, is also self-love. It is pride that wants to possess more than others.

What about lust? It is self-love, pride aspiring to be tops in self-gratification.

To be "poor in spirit" means to give God first place, to love Him most, to go His way. Jesus said, "My Father, if it is possible, may this cup be taken from Me. Yet not as I will, but as You will" (Matthew 26:39). Jesus drank the cup of God's wrath for you and me when He suffered and died on the cross for all our sins, including our sinful pride. God's love for us motivates us to be rich by being poor in spirit. Recognizing our failures and shortcomings, we will joyfully claim Christ's redeeming grace.

Humility leads us to God's Word for guidance. The proud think they know it all and rely on themselves. Through faith in Jesus, the poor in spirit realize their limitations, ask for and richly receive God's help.

Prayer: Dear Lord, You taught me that the low are lifted high. Amen.

Blessed are those who mourn, for they will be comforted. Matthew 5:4

Tears for the Lost

Jesus wept bitter tears over the city that had become a harlot. "He wept over [Jerusalem] and said, 'If you, even you, had only known on this day what would bring you peace—but now it is hidden from your eyes' " (Luke 19:41–42).

Nearest the heart of Jesus, then and now, is His concern for the eternal salvation of all. "The Son of Man came to seek and to save what was lost" (Luke 19:10). As then, Jesus still mourns over those who by their unbelief are signing their own death warrant.

Jesus wants us to mourn too. We should mourn over the supertragedy of those who are turning away from His grace, rejecting His offer of salvation, and instead choosing judgment and death.

The prophet Isaiah has this plaintive message: "Why spend money on what is not bread, and your labor on what does not satisfy?" (Isaiah 55:2).

Those who truly mourn over what the world has come to will find great joy in what has come into the world through our Savior.

Prayer: Lord, it is by Your grace that we learn to mourn over those who are lost and pray for their salvation. Amen.

*Blessed are the meek, for they will inherit
the earth. Matthew 5:5*

How Rich You Are!

Jesus explicitly states that through gentleness we inherit the earth. This is a superlative promise. God wants us to put the full weight of our trust in this promise. He makes it clear and pledges unconditionally that a meek and gentle person will inherit the earth.

The apostle Paul helps us to understand in what sense the meek inherit the earth: "All things are yours … and you are of Christ, and Christ is of God" (1Corinthians 3:21, 23). Through His death, Jesus made us to be sons of God; and as sons of God we are given the right to be heirs of His. "To those who believed in His name, He gave the right to become children of God" (John 1:12). All things are God's, we are His, so all things are ours. We inherit the best there is in the world.

May God enable us through faith in Christ Jesus to be gentle and meek enough to believe from the heart that no one in all the world is richer than we are or enjoys God more than we do.

Prayer: O Holy Spirit, help us to be meek and gentle, making us richer than the richest. Amen.

*Blessed are the merciful, for they
will be shown mercy. Matthew 5:7*

Lord, Give Me a Loving Concern for Others

Jesus was a merciful person. He had warm sympathy for people, especially those in trouble. Probably many times He said, "Come to Me, all you who are weary and burdened, and I will give you rest" (Matthew 11:28). To us as His followers Jesus says, "Be merciful, just as your Father is merciful" (Luke 6:36). In other words, God's mercy, demonstrated through His Son's death on the cross, should inspire our mercy.

If we could make a list of all the mercies that the heavenly Father has showered upon us, we would exclaim jubilantly, "Dear Lord, we thank and praise You for all Your mercies!"

Jesus said, "From everyone who has been given much, much will be demanded; and from the one who has been entrusted with much, much more will be asked" (Luke 12:48). We who have received God's mercy, grace, and goodness are empowered to be merciful and charity-minded. We have many opportunities that invite our compassion and mercy. We can readily draw up a list of people who are poor, hungry, distressed, sick, cold, lonely. True, we cannot help everyone, but we can help some.

We can be very sure of this: "Blessed are the merciful, for they will be shown mercy."

Prayer: Dear Lord, enriched by Your mercy, help me to be merciful by showing a loving concern for others. Amen.

Blessed are the pure in heart,
for they will see God.
Matthew 5:8

A Happy, Holy Heart

By the grace of God we have a new, clean heart. We show this in our everyday life by pursuing what is pure and holy, clean and true.

This doesn't come easy. We are living in a contaminated climate. We are exposed to a polluted culture. Worst of all, within ourselves we have a defiled heart.

It's always been this way. In Old Testament times the psalmist David, after committing a heinous sin, pleaded with God, "Create in me a pure heart, O God" (Psalm 51:10).

Where does all the moral perversion come from? It comes out of our sin-diseased human heart. We, like David, can through faith in Jesus confess our sin and be assured that "if we confess our sins, He [God] is faithful and just and will forgive us our sins and purify us" (1 John 1:9). A heart cleansed by the blood of Jesus is able to love all that is virtuous. It chooses edifying books to read, clean shows to see, helpful television programs to view, worthwhile conversations to engage in, right and ennobling thoughts to think, good and fine people to meet, upright and decent things to do.

Prayer: "Create in me a pure heart, O God, and renew a steadfast spirit within me" (Psalm 51:10). Amen.

Be joyful always; pray continually; give thanks in all circumstances, for this is God's will for you in Christ Jesus. 1 Thessalonians 5:16–17

Never Give Up Praying

It is certainly true that through prayer we can draw God's blessings down upon many people and causes; and if we don't do it, it doesn't speak well of us.

When Jesus suffered and died for us, He earned for us the privilege of approaching God as our Father. Through Christ we "received the Spirit of sonship. And by Him we cry, 'Abba, Father' " (Romans 8:15).

God commands us to "pray continually" (1 Thessalonians 5:17). Prayer is a mystery beyond our understanding, but not beyond our faith. God promises that He will answer every prayer that comes to Him through faith. Every day offers multiple opportunities to pray fervently, frequently, extensively, joyfully, and confidently to God for all things.

Prayer: Dear God, help me to think of all the good You can accomplish through my prayers in order that I may be encouraged to pray more. Amen.

Then I saw a new heaven and a new earth.
Revelation 21:1

The Beauty and Glory of the Holy City

The Holy Spirit employs the rich splendor of jewels to symbolize the beauty of the city of God.

> The foundations of the city walls were decorated with every kind of precious stone. The first foundation was jasper, the second sapphire, the third chalcedony, the fourth emerald, the fifth sardonyx, the sixth carnelian, the seventh chrysolite, the eighth beryl, the ninth topaz, the tenth chrysoprase, the eleventh jacinth, and the twelfth amethyst" (Revelation 21: 19–20).

Jasper is white tinged with green; sapphire is blue; chalcedony (agate) is fire red; emerald is green; sardonyx is red with white veins; chrysolite is bright gold; beryl is aqua; topaz is brownish yellow; chrysoprase is greenish with gold; jacinth is yellow with red; amethyst is violet.

Twelve doors lead into this holy palace, each door being one single pearl. Each pearl door stands for the Lord Jesus Christ, who said, "I am the way. … No one comes to the Father except through Me" (John 14:6).

There is the tree of Life in the new paradise of heaven. Just as by one tree Satan overcame the world, so by one tree, the cross, Jesus overcame Satan. In the tree of Life there is healing.

Prayer: O Holy Spirit, keep us all in Christ that we may be citizens of Your holy city forever. Amen.

PART III

Prayers

Pray continually.
1 Thessalonians 5:16

For a Better Life

Lord God, create in me a clean heart and renew a right spirit within me. Because You have called me to Your side to sing Your praises and to glorify Your name, I earnestly desire that my life may be higher than its surroundings. When I see the hurt and pain that follows sin, I realize that sin is my enemy as well as Yours.

Lord, I want to wholly yield to Your will. In Your Son You provided a way out of sin and its curse, out of death and its darkness, out of the power of Satan and his fury, out of the anguish and terror of hell; You have given me Your hand to hold, Your way to walk, Your love to show, Your humility to exhibit, Your promises to trust, and Your presence to enjoy. In Jesus' name I thank You. Amen.

For Joy in Living

Lord Jesus, grant that all through this day my heart may be filled with the joy of salvation. On the darkest night of Your life You prayed that Your children might have Your joy and Your peace. Because of what You did for me on the cross, grant me the joy beyond all telling, the peace beyond all understanding, the golden hope beyond all describing.

Let Your love set my spirit ablaze with praise and thanksgiving. Let faith, love, joy, and hope so fill my heart and spirit that there will be no room left for gloom, doubt, fear, or discouragement.

It is my earnest hope and sincere resolution that in all things I say and do, You will be glorified. In the light and power of Your presence, let me preach the living sermon of contentment under Your care, joy in Your grace, trust in Your promises and hope in Your salvation. I pray in Your holy name. Amen.

For Joy in the Redeemed Life

Lord Jesus, You redeemed me not with gold or silver but with Your holy, precious blood and innocent suffering and death. Through the Holy Spirit You called me into Your Kingdom and adopted me as a member of God's holy family.

Lord, this day and every day of my life I desire to walk on redemption ground, live in redemption joy, glory in redemption grace. It is my hope and desire to live the redemption life, to have the redemption look, to exhibit the redemption spirit, to share the redemption story, and to march toward redemption glory.

Attune my spirit to the holy truth that I am a redeemed, forgiven, loved, cherished, honored child of God on my way to everlasting life in the new world. I pray this, dear Jesus, in Your Name and to your glory. Amen.

For a Life of Service

Lord Jesus, You changed my future from death to life, from dread to delight, from darkness to light, from damnation to celebration, from eternal pain to eternal gain. For this I thank You and praise You.

Let me serve You in the beauty of holiness. Grant that this day may be a productive, fruitful day. Let my faith glow, my love shine, my spirit sing, my lips teach, my heart rejoice, my tongue declare Your goodness and glory. I ask it on the ground of Your grace and to Your everlasting glory. Amen.

Prayers of Peace

Lord God, thank You for the heavenly and holy gift of peace. I know that true and abiding peace flows from the cross on which the Prince of Glory died. On this old rugged cross the armistice between God and man has been signed in the blood of the Prince of Peace. Help me and all Your children to understand what a precious boon is ours through the gift of peace. I pray in Jesus' name. Amen.

Lord Jesus, like a clock ticking in the thunderstorm, Your peace remains serene and constant in the midst of life's storms. I thank and praise You for coming to me many times a day with Your precious greeting; "peace be to you." Out of the abundance of Your peace grant me the grace to be one of those blessed peacemakers who shall see God. In Jesus' holy name. Amen.

O God, from whom all holy desires, all good counsels, and all just works proceed, give to Your servants that peace which the world cannot give that our hearts may be set to obey Your commandments and also that we, being defended by You, may pass our time in rest and quietness; through the merits of Jesus Christ, our Savior. Amen. (*LW*, p. 129)